D1406510

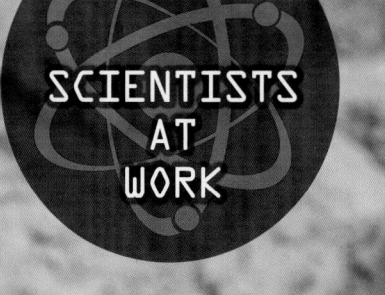

SCIENTISTS
AT
WORK

Anthropologists
at Work

THERESE M. SHEA

Britannica®
Educational Publishing

IN ASSOCIATION WITH

ROSEN
EDUCATIONAL SERVICES

Published in 2018 by Britannica Educational Publishing (a trademark of Encyclopædia Britannica, Inc.) in association with The Rosen Publishing Group, Inc.
29 East 21st Street, New York, NY 10010

Copyright © 2018 The Rosen Publishing Group, Inc. and Encyclopædia Britannica, Inc. Encyclopaedia Britannica, Britannica, and the Thistle logo are registered trademarks of Encyclopædia Britannica, Inc. All rights reserved.

Distributed exclusively by Rosen Publishing.
To see additional Britannica Educational Publishing titles, go to rosenpublishing.com.

First Edition

Britannica Educational Publishing
J.E. Luebering: Executive Director, Core Editorial
Mary Rose McCudden: Editor, Britannica Student Encyclopedia

Rosen Publishing
Nicholas Croce: Editor
Nelson Sá: Art Director
Nicole Russo-Duca: Designer
Cindy Reiman: Photography Manager
Nicole Baker: Photo Researcher

Library of Congress Cataloging-in-Publication Data

Names: Shea, Therese, author.
Title: Anthropologists at work / Therese M. Shea.
Description: First edition. | New York : Britannica Educational Publishing,
[2018] | Series: Scientists at work | Includes bibliographical references
and index. | Audience: Grade 1 to 4.
Identifiers: LCCN 2016053923| ISBN 9781680487428 (6 pack : alk. paper) | ISBN 9781680487435 (library bound
book : alk. paper) | ISBN 9781680487411 (pbk. book : alk. paper)
Subjects: LCSH: Anthropologists—Juvenile literature. |
Anthropology—Juvenile literature.
Classification: LCC GN31.5 .S54 2017 | DDC 301—dc23
LC record available at https://lccn.loc.gov/2016053923

Manufactured in the United States of America

Photo credits: Cover, p. 1 Microgen/Shutterstock.com; pp. 4, 5 Encyclopaedia Britannica, Inc.; p. 6 Gianni Tortoli/ Science Source/Getty Images; p. 7 © Comstock/Thinkstock; p. 8 William Campbell/Sygma/Getty Images; p. 9 Cleveland Museum of Natural History; p. 10 Tek Image/Science Photo Library/Getty Images; p. 11 © deanm1974/ Fotolia; p. 12 Alllexxxis; p. 13 Marilyn Angel Wynn/Nativestock/Getty Images; p. 14 Courtesy of the Rijksmuseum, Amsterdam, purchased with the support of the F.G. Waller-Fonds; p. 15 PeopleImages/DigitalVision/Getty Images; p. 16 Library of Congress, Washington, D.C. (neg. no. LC-USZ62-95224); p. 17 © ChiccoDodiFC/Fotolia; p. 18 Adrian Pingstone; p. 19 Jim Sugar/Corbis Documentary/Getty Images; p. 20 Andrew Lichtenstein/Corbis News/ Getty Images; p. 21 © Photos.com/Jupiterimages; p. 22 Jeffery L. Rotman/Corbis Documentary/Getty Images; p. 23 Wolfgang Kaehler/LightRocket/Getty Images; p. 24 Diane Macdonald/Photodisc/Getty Images; p. 25 Library of Congress/Corbis Historical/Getty Images; p. 26 © Photos.com/Jupiterimages/Thinkstock; p. 27 Rex Features/ AP Images; p. 28 © Franz Aberham-Digital Vision/Getty Images; p. 29 DEA/A. Dagli Orti/De Agostini/Getty Images; interior pages background Iryna Potapenko/Shutterstock.com.

Contents

Connecting with the Past

Scientists have long wondered when human intelligence—our unique ability to think and learn—first developed. Certain scientists tried to answer that question by studying the remains of early human ancestors. The scientists were able to compare some skulls of the early ancestors with the skulls of modern humans. The scientists discovered that the brains of humans increased in size over time. The scientists think the increased brain size led to modern human intelligence. What type of scientist would research such a topic? An anthropologist would.

Anthropology is the study of human beings and their cultures, from prehistoric times

The brains of human ancestors increased in size over time. Scientists think this led to modern human intelligence.

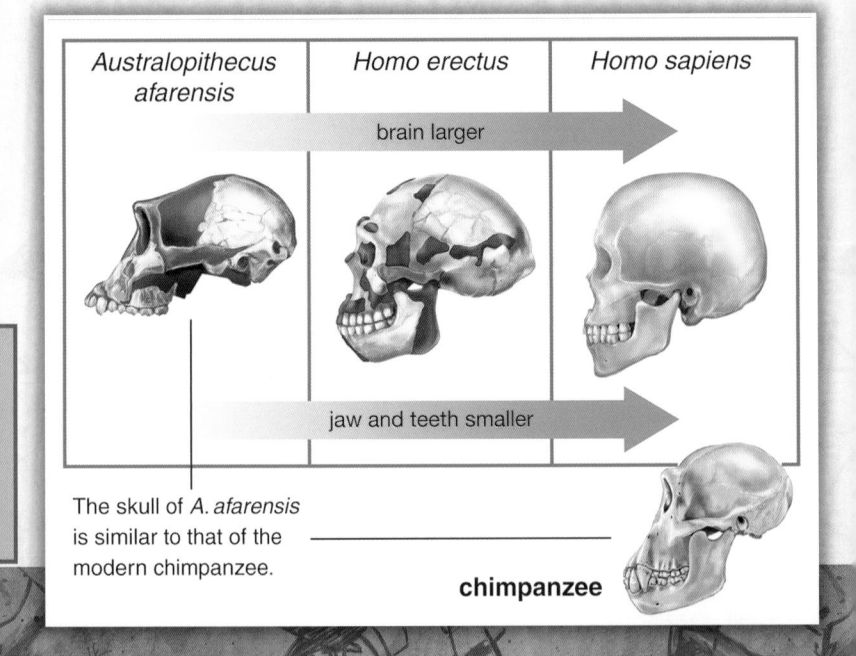

Australopithecus afarensis

Homo erectus

Homo sapiens

brain larger

jaw and teeth smaller

The skull of *A. afarensis* is similar to that of the modern chimpanzee.

chimpanzee

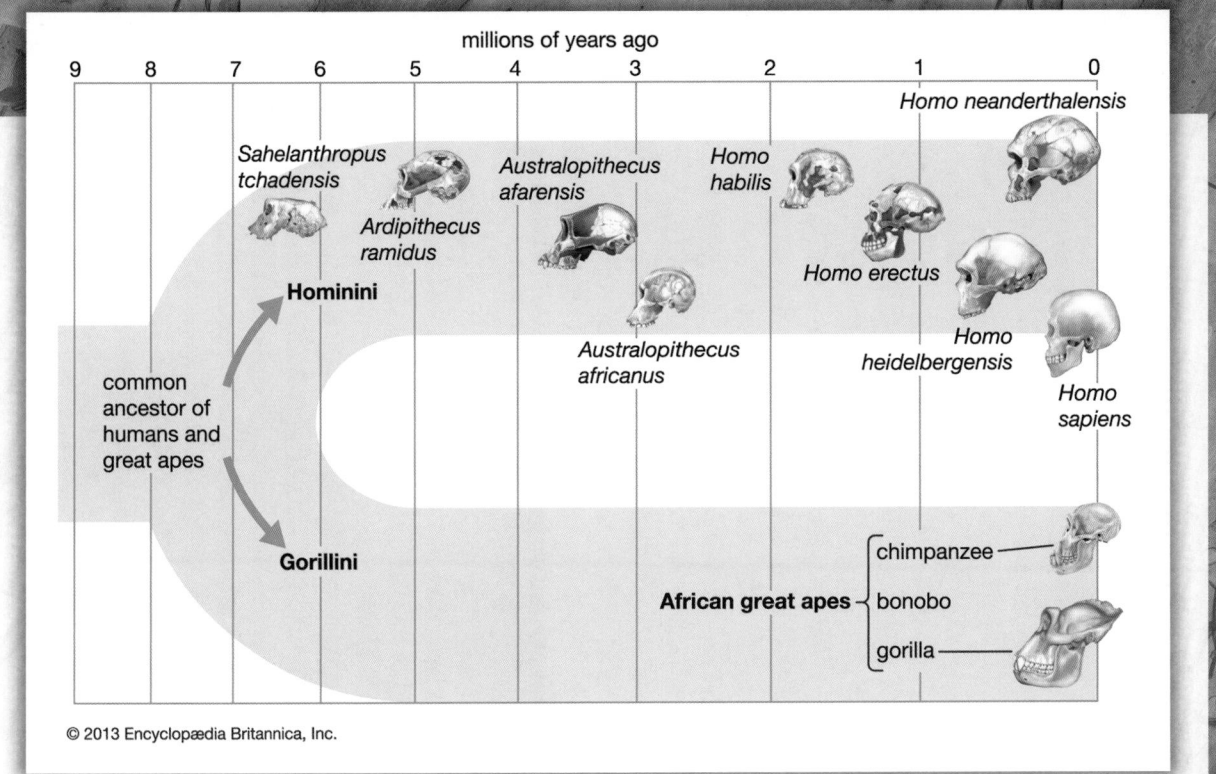

millions of years ago

9　8　7　6　5　4　3　2　1　0

Homo neanderthalensis

Sahelanthropus tchadensis

Ardipithecus ramidus

Australopithecus afarensis

Homo habilis

Hominini

Australopithecus africanus

Homo erectus

Homo heidelbergensis

Homo sapiens

common ancestor of humans and great apes

Gorillini

African great apes — chimpanzee — bonobo — gorilla

© 2013 Encyclopædia Britannica, Inc.

This graph shows that it took millions of years for both modern humans and great apes to develop from an apelike ancestor.

to today. Anthropologists often compare different human communities to find out their similarities and differences. By doing this, anthropologists hope to increase knowledge about humanity as a whole, as well as about certain groups of people.

THINK ABOUT IT

How does intelligence make humans unique among animals on this planet?

Branches of Anthropology

Anthropology is often divided into two main branches: physical anthropology and cultural anthropology. Physical anthropologists study the physical features of humans. Cultural anthropologists study human cultures. Cultures are the shared beliefs and practices of groups of people. Both of these kinds of anthropology may include the study of prehistoric, ancient, and modern humans.

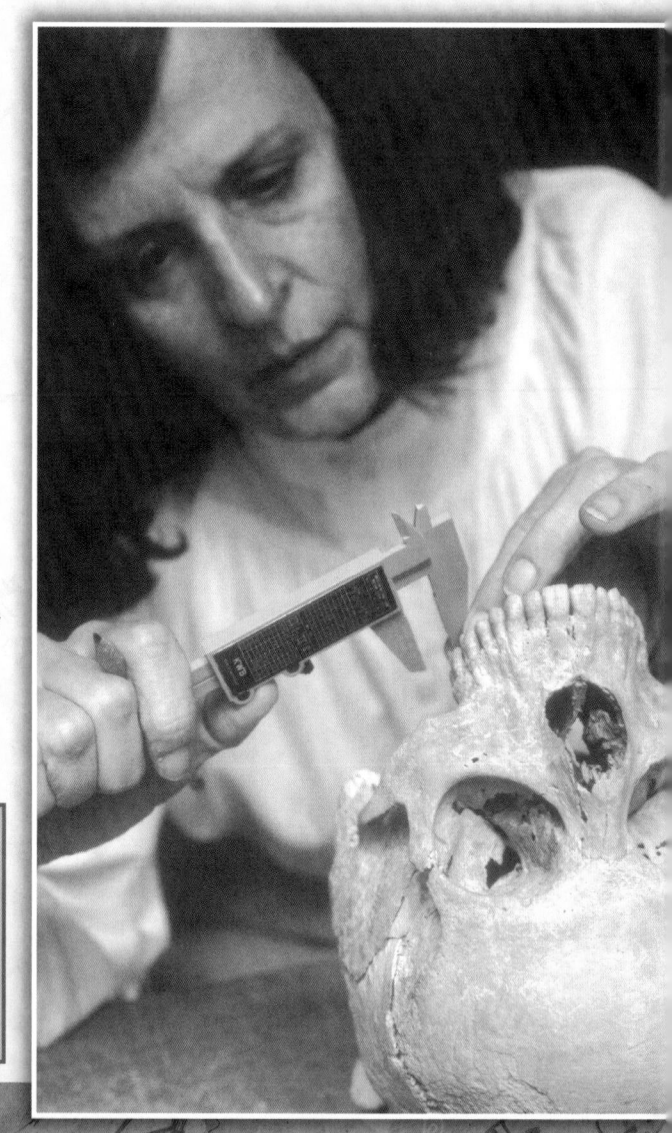

A physical anthropologist measures a skull of someone who lived in ancient Greece some 2,500 years ago.

Physically, people of different races and ethnicities have more similarities than differences even though cultural differences can be great.

Anthropologists often focus on certain time periods.

It is common for physical and cultural anthropologists to work with each other to provide a complete picture of a period in human history. For example, cultural anthropologists may study artifacts to tell us about the way humans lived, while physical anthropologists can examine a skeleton to tell us when and how that person died.

COMPARE AND CONTRAST

What do you think are some challenges of studying the humans of prehistoric, ancient, and modern times?

Physical Anthropology

Physical anthropology is deeply connected to biology, or the science of life. It is also called biological anthropology. Physical anthropologists examine and measure physical traits in living humans as well as in human fossils. Some physical anthropologists compare the physical features among people from different areas. They consider why people have different features. Other physical anthropologists research what makes humans physically different from other animals, such as apes and monkeys.

Some physical anthropologists study the remains of prehistoric humans to learn about human origins. They

Anthropologist Richard Leakey poses with the skull of a human ancestor called *Australopithecus*.

Anthropologist Donald Johanson found the skeleton of a human ancestor called *Australopithecus afarensis* in Ethiopia in 1974. The skeleton is nicknamed Lucy. It is more than three million years old.

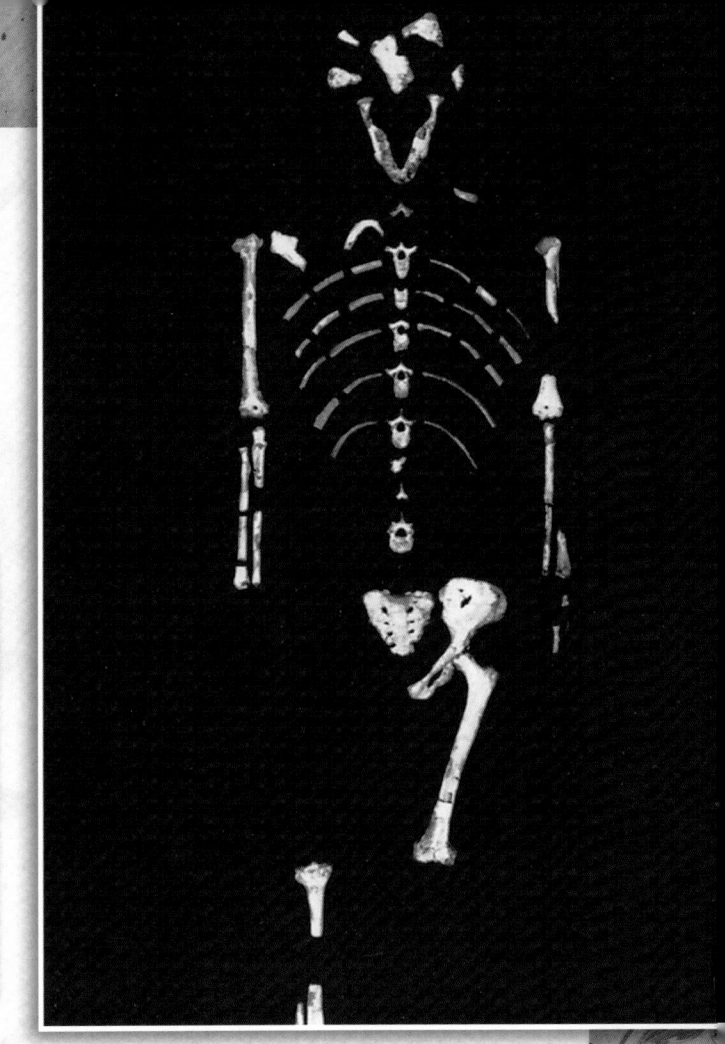

VOCABULARY

Evolution is the idea that all living things develop from earlier forms of life. These changes happen by a natural process over a very long time.

are called paleoanthropologists. They try to find out how and when modern humans developed from early forms of humans and from nonhuman ancestors. In other words, they study human **evolution**.

All humans have the same genes arranged in the same order. The differences within genes are what make us unique. This image shows a sample of a person's "genetic fingerprint."

VOCABULARY

Primates are members of the group of mammals that contains human beings, apes, and monkeys.

Physical anthropologists are also interested in how human behavior is connected to human biology. They measure the shape, size, and structure of physical features, but they do not just examine bones. They often study human genes. These are the units within cells that pass along traits from parents to children. Anthropologists may compare genes between different populations of humans or between humans and other **primates.**

Children inherit traits from their parents. Scientists study genes to find out how that happens. The study of genetics can also help show how groups of people are related.

The study of genes has helped show how and when groups of people have moved from one area to another throughout history. Anthropologists also look at blood types to learn about the movements of early peoples. Blood has certain features that vary from person to person. People can be grouped according to the features that they share.

Cultural Anthropology

Cultural anthropology is a social science, or a field of study focused on human societies. Cultural anthropologists study all parts of human cultures, in all different places and times. These may include art, language (linguistics), religion, clothing, customs, and social structure. Cultural anthropologists also compare the practices of various societies. Some traditions are practiced by many groups of people, whereas other traditions

Funeral practices, such as those shown here in Bali, are among the customs and rituals that cultural anthropologists study.

may be practiced by just one group.

Anthropologists do not judge a culture's practices as good or bad. Instead, they try to find out what the practices mean to the people of that culture and when those practices began.

A Native American in Alaska continues the tradition of storytelling that has been important in his culture for generations.

THINK ABOUT IT

Famous anthropologist Margaret Mead studied different groups of people on islands in the Pacific Ocean. She found that women and men behave as their culture teaches them and that they are not born with ideas of how to act. Do you think this is true? Why or why not?

A Newer Science

Anthropology is a newer science that took shape in the mid-1800s. Around that time, advances in other sciences helped support the **scientific theories** of naturalist Charles Darwin. In his 1859 book *On the Origin of Species,*

VOCABULARY

A **scientific theory** is an explanation for why things work or how things happen. It is based on ideas that can be tested.

Charles Darwin's theories were quite shocking in his time, and many people refused to accept them.

Darwin stated that all species, including humans, developed from earlier forms. Darwin further declared that a defining feature in humans is brain size. He concluded that intelligence helped humans survive.

Scientists became interested in how living things change. Anthropologists became interested in how humans change and how they develop culture.

Some scientists today argue that race is more of a social concept than one based on biology because everyone's genes are so similar.

Some theories in anthropology have been proven wrong. Anthropologists once divided people into races based on traits such as skin color. In the late twentieth century, anthropologists found that modern humans are all very similar in their genes. In fact, there is no scientific basis for dividing people into races.

Important Theories

ON

THE ORIGIN OF SPECIES

BY MEANS OF NATURAL SELECTION,

OR THE

PRESERVATION OF FAVOURED RACES IN THE STRUGGLE
FOR LIFE.

By CHARLES DARWIN, M.A.,

FELLOW OF THE ROYAL, GEOLOGICAL, LINNÆAN, ETC., SOCIETIES;
AUTHOR OF 'JOURNAL OF RESEARCHES DURING H. M. S. BEAGLE'S VOYAGE
ROUND THE WORLD.'

LONDON:
JOHN MURRAY, ALBEMARLE STREET.
1859.

The right of Translation is reserved.

Darwin's theory became known as evolution. It was important to both physical and cultural anthropology. By examining the fossils of human ancestors, physical anthropologists can see how human ancestors changed physically over time. Cultural anthropologists used the idea of evolution to explain how all cultures develop in stages over time.

Physical anthropology is related to the science of biology. It is supported by scientific theories that often can

Charles Darwin's work *On the Origin of Species* is still studied today, and his theories have become important principles in other branches of science.

Irrigation was one of the developments that marked the great ancient civilizations of the world. Its origin is unclear.

be tested and are accepted by most scientists. Cultural anthropology is a social science. It is supported by theories that are more difficult to prove.

Theories in cultural anthropology try to explain how human culture develops. For example, one theory states that each culture is unique because of its unique location, history, and encounters with other cultures. Another theory explains that all cultures developed from one early civilization, such as ancient Egypt.

COMPARE AND CONTRAST

Which of the theories described here are convincing to you? Which do you disagree with? Why?

Digging Up History

Different kinds of anthropologists collect information in different ways. An archaeologist is a kind of anthropologist that studies things that people made, used, and left behind. Archaeologists want to understand what people were like and how they lived. An archaeologist's work begins with finding a site to study. Some sites are visible on the surface. Sometimes archaeologists must use technology such as radar to find sites that are buried underground.

Excavations can unearth objects that prove or disprove theories. Sometimes the objects cause anthropologists to develop new theories altogether.

After finding a site, an archaeologist digs slowly and carefully. This work is called excavation, or a "dig." Archaeologists use spoons, knives, picks, brushes, and other tools in their work. They try to uncover bones, buildings, tools, weapons, art, and any other artifacts.

Anthropologists study objects that are important clues to understanding a culture. For example, rocks were shaped into tools by some ancient peoples.

THINK ABOUT IT

Why do you think an archaeologist digs slowly and carefully after finding a site?

Archaeologists have discovered that some paintings made on cave walls in Europe and South Africa are thousands of years old. They found this by using carbon-14 dating on the pigments used to make the paintings.

Archaeologists have several methods for figuring out an artifact's age. One method is called carbon-14 dating. Carbon-14 is a chemical found in all organisms, or living things. After an organism dies, the amount of carbon-14 decreases at a certain rate. Scientists can measure this decrease to find out how long ago the organism died.

Carbon-14 dating cannot be used to measure the age of things that are more than one hundred thousand years old.

This stone artifact was excavated from a site in Egypt. It is believed to be from about 2200 BCE. It shows a person in the process of brewing beer.

Other chemicals can be used for older remains and for objects that did not come from living things. Potassium-argon dating, for example, can be used on rock tools that are millions of years old.

Anthropologists also try to understand the culture from which artifacts came. For example, tools such as arrow tips, knives, and grinding stones can reveal what and how people ate.

COMPARE AND CONTRAST

What kind of dating would be helpful for finding out how old a skeleton is? What about a spear point?

Not Just the Past

In the 1800s and early 1900s, most cultural anthropologists were from western Europe or the United States. They usually traveled to another part of the world, such as Africa or Asia, to study different cultures.

Today, cultural anthropologists from all around the world study a wide variety of human groups, including their own cultures. For instance, they may study small fishing villages,

A cultural anthropologist learns from a Bedouin man. Bedouins live in the deserts of the Middle East and North Africa, moving often in search of water and food.

Linguistic anthropologists may travel far to hear languages they are interested in. This anthropologist listens to native people in West New Guinea.

gangs in big cities, religious groups, or large companies.

Cultural anthropologists might go to a place to interview people about their culture. They also might live among a group of people for a time, sometimes for months or even years, to observe the culture in action.

THINK ABOUT IT

Why do you think anthropologists might choose to observe rather than do interviews to learn about a culture?

Listening to Languages

Linguistics is the study of the history and structure of language. It is especially important to cultural anthropologists. Linguistic anthropologists believe that spoken and written languages help form human cultures.

Thousands of languages are spoken in the world today. Linguistic anthropologists try to explain why there are so many and why some languages become extinct while others live on. They are interested in how people learn languages. They also

Many cultures are attempting to keep their local languages alive, even when most of the people speak a more common language. This sign in Scotland is written in both English and Gaelic.

Welcome to the Highlands
Fàilte don Ghàidhealtachd

This chart shows the alphabet for the writing system of the Cherokee language. The system was developed by Sequoyah, a Cherokee leader of the early nineteenth century.

THINK ABOUT IT

Signs, books, letters, and websites all contain written language. How do you think social media helps form human culture today?

Cherokee Alphabet

Sounds represented by vowels.

Consonant Sounds.

study why there are differences within a language. Most people in England and the United States speak the English language, but they don't always use the same words in the same ways. For example, a "lift" in England is an "elevator" in the United States.

Linguistic anthropologists may also live among people whose language is dying out in order to record the language before it becomes extinct.

Anthropology in the News

Anthropologists make interesting discoveries all the time. In 2015 several such finds made the news. An archaeologist found evidence of hidden chambers in the tomb of Egyptian pharaoh Tutankhamen, popularly known as "King Tut." Several cities belonging to a previously unknown culture were found in a rainforest in Central America. People lived in the cities one thousand years ago.

A new human ancestor was identified from remains found in a cave in South Africa. The remains

Because few Egyptian tombs have survived as intact as the pharaoh Tutankhamen's, the public has been fascinated by him and his tomb's treasures.

VOCABULARY

A **species** is a group of related living things that share common features and are able to produce young with one another.

were from at least fifteen males and females of various ages. The **species**, *Homo naledi*, appears to have walked upright, as *Homo sapiens*—humans—do. Anthropologists will continue to study the fossils to learn more about how the species lived.

New technologies have helped anthropologists and other scientists to make these discoveries. Undoubtedly, more breakthroughs and theories are on the horizon.

The bones of *Homo naledi* are pictured here. Anthropologists found more than 1,500 bones in the South African cave.

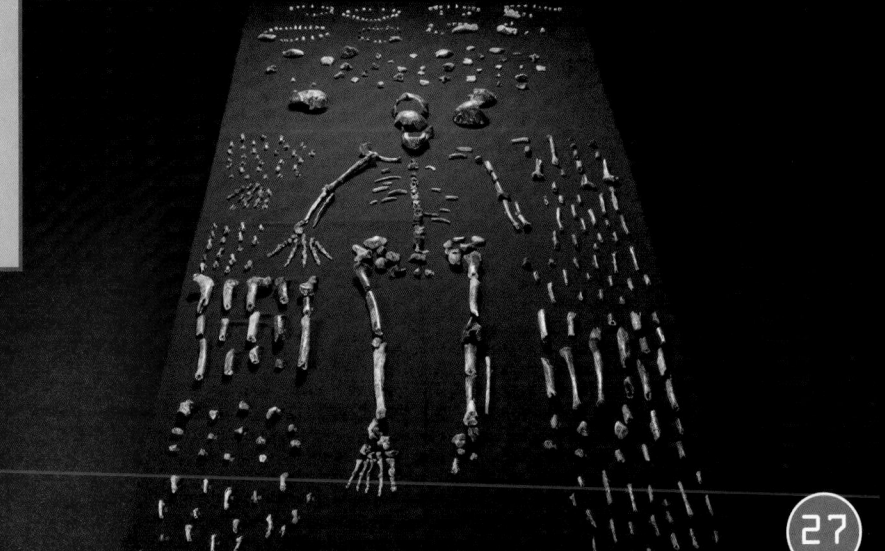

The Complete Picture

Margaret Mead was one of the most famous anthropologists of the 1900s. She is best known for her studies of the island peoples of Oceania in the Pacific Ocean. Mead wrote that anthropology demands "the open-mindedness with which one must look and listen." She meant that anthropologists must be open to new ways of thinking that are different from their own.

Anthropologists investigate human societies, past and present—in even the smallest detail. The field of anthropology

Anthropologists will continue to find evidence of past life, such as these cave paintings, and try to understand what they mean to the continuing story of humankind.

These ancient artifacts, made of bone, were shaped and decorated for a purpose. Anthropologists try to discover that purpose and make connections among cultures.

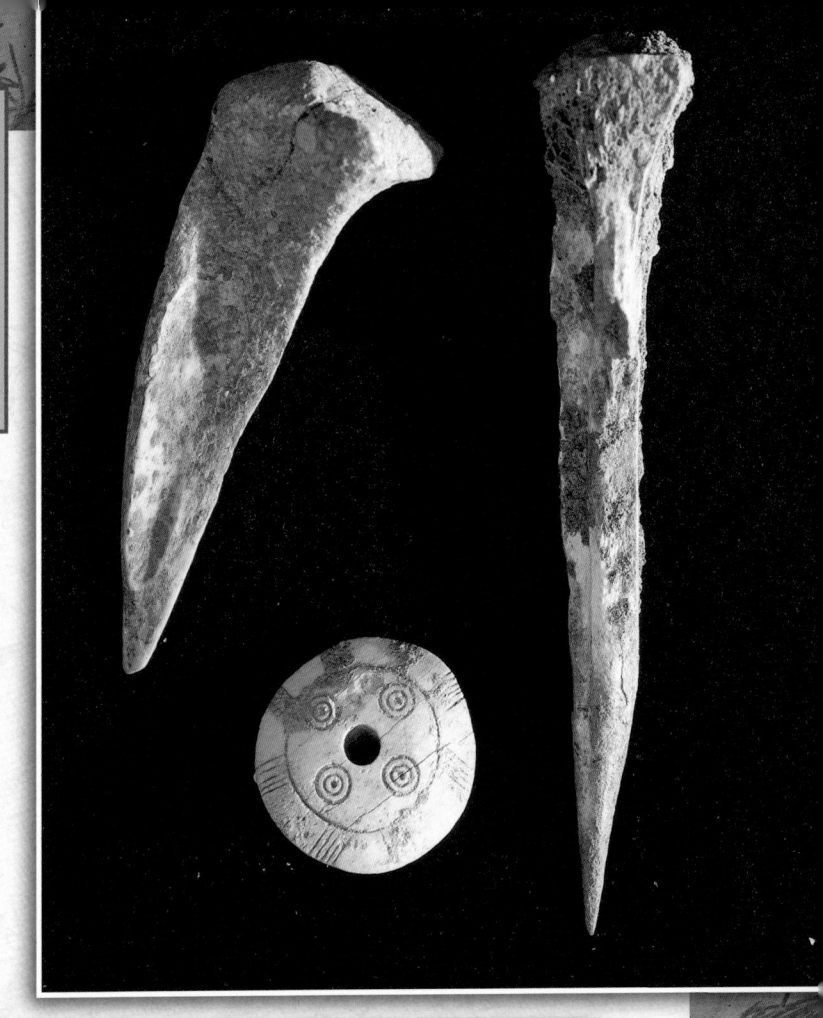

draws upon history, geography, geology, biology, anatomy, genetics, and other subjects for a complete picture. Such a vast field requires that anyone studying it ask questions, listen closely, and keep an open mind.

THINK ABOUT IT

How might your experiences affect the way you see a culture? How might you deal with that if you were an anthropologist?

Glossary

ANATOMY A branch of biology that deals with the structures that make up the bodies of living things.

ANCESTOR One from whom an individual, group, or species is descended.

ANCIENT Of or relating to a period of time long past.

ARTIFACT A usually simple object showing human work and representing a culture or a stage in the development of a culture.

CHEMICAL A substance obtained from a chemical process or used to change another substance.

EXTINCT No longer existing.

FOSSIL A trace or remain of a plant or animal that lived long ago.

GEOLOGY The study of the physical features and history of Earth.

INTELLIGENCE The ability to learn, understand, or deal with problems.

PERSONALITY The set of emotional qualities or ways of behaving that makes a person different from others.

PHARAOH A ruler of ancient Egypt.

PREHISTORIC Of, relating to, or existing in times before written history.

RADAR A radio device for detecting the position of things in the distance.

RESEARCH The collecting of information about a particular subject.

SOCIAL MEDIA Forms of electronic communication through which people create online communities to share information, ideas, and messages.

TECHNOLOGY The use of knowledge to invent new devices or tools; also the devices and tools that are invented.

TRAIT An inherited characteristic.

UNIQUE Being the only one of its kind.

For More Information

Books

Aronson, Marc, and Lee R. Berger. *The Skull in the Rock: How a Scientist, a Boy, and Google Earth Opened a New Window on Human Origins*. Washington, DC: National Geographic, 2012.

Ganeri, Anita, and David West. *The Curse of King Tut's Tomb and Other Ancient Discoveries*. New York, NY: Rosen Publishing Group, 2012.

Latta, Sara L. *Bones: Dead People DO Tell Tales*. Berkeley Heights, NJ: Enslow Publishers, 2012.

Noon, Steve. *A Street Through Time*. New York, NY: DK Publishing, 2012.

Weaver, Anne H., and Matt Celeskey. *Children of Time: Evolution and the Human Story*. Albuquerque, NM: University of New Mexico Press, 2012.

Websites

Because of the changing nature of internet links, Rosen Publishing has developed an online list of websites related to the subject of this book. This site is updated regularly. Please use this link to access the list:

http://www.rosenlinks.com/SAW/anthro

Index